Class Treats, Bake Sales & Birthday Parties

A Mom's Recipe Book

Printed in the United States of America
by G&R Publishing Co.

Distributed By:

507 Industrial Street
Waverly, IA 50677

ISBN 1-56383-138-4
Item #7020

Table of Contents

Spring

Birdhouse Cupcakes

Makes 12 cupcakes

12 paper baking cups
1/2 C. butter or margarine, softened
3/4 C. sugar
1 tsp. ground cinnamon
1/2 tsp. baking soda
1/2 tsp. ground nutmeg
1/2 tsp. vanilla
1/4 tsp. salt
2 eggs
1 C. mashed overripe bananas
  (about 3 medium)
1 (8 oz.) can crushed pineapple in juice,
  well drained
1 1/3 C. all-purpose flour
6 T. butter or margarine, softened
1 (8 oz.) pkg. cream cheese, softened
3 1/2 C. powdered sugar
Green, blue, pink and yellow paste
  (gel) food color
12 thin pretzel sticks
12 semi-sweet chocolate mini Kisses
Tiny flower candies

Preheat the oven to 375°F. Line 12 muffin cups with baking cups.

In a large bowl, beat butter, sugar, cinnamon, baking soda, nutmeg, vanilla and salt with mixer on high speed for 1 minute or until well blended. Add eggs; beat for 2 minutes or until fluffy. Reduce speed to low; beat in bananas and pineapple (batter will look curdled), then add flour just until blended. Spoon into lined muffin cups (they'll be full).

Bake 18 to 22 minutes until a toothpick inserted in centers comes out clean. Cool in pan on a wire rack for 5 minutes, then remove cupcakes from pan to rack to cool completely.

To make frosting, beat butter, cream cheese and powdered sugar in a large bowl with mixer on low speed until blended. Increase speed to high; beat for 2 minutes or until smooth and fluffy.

Tint 1/4 cup frosting green and spoon into a plastic bag; set aside. Divide remaining frosting among 3 cups and tint blue, pink and yellow. Cover tightly until ready to use.

Peel liners off cupcakes; place on a flat tray. Working with 1 color frosting at a time, drop a heaping teaspoon on 4 cupcakes; spoon remainder into a plastic bag. Snip 1/8" tip off corner of bag and pipe lines of frosting to simulate thatch for roof. Snip tip off corner of bag with green frosting and pipe grass around base of cupcakes. Insert pretzels and Kisses (point first); press flowers on grass tops.

Easy Easter Nests

Makes 24 servings

2 T. butter or margarine
3 C. miniature marshmallows
4 C. fruit-flavored crispy rice cereal
Coconut
Assorted candies

Microwave butter in large microwavable bowl on high 30 seconds or until melted. Add marshmallows; toss to coat. Microwave 1 1/2 minutes, stirring after 45 seconds. Add cereal; toss lightly to coat well.

Press mixture firmly into lightly greased muffin pan to form 24 nests; cool.

Fill nests with coconut and candies.

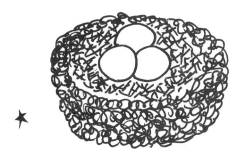

Easter Bonnets

Makes 12 servings

1 (18 oz.) pkg. refrigerated
   sugar cookie dough
12 purchased lemon or
   orange mini muffins
1 (16 oz.) tub vanilla frosting
Green and red food color

Using slice and bake method, bake and cool 12 cookies as directed on cookie wrapper. Reserve remaining dough for a later use.

If necessary, remove tops from muffins. Cut 3/4" slice off bottom of each muffin to use for bonnet. Reserve muffin tops for snacking. Spread cut side of each muffin bottom with frosting; attach to cookie, frosting side down. Place bonnets on rack set over baking pan.

Place 1/2 cup frosting in resealable plastic bag. Add green food color; squeeze bag until well mixed and of desired color.

Place remaining frosting in microwave safe measuring cup with pouring spout. Microwave on high for 30 to 40 seconds or until pourable. Do not boil. Stir in enough red food color for desired pink color.

Pour pink frosting over bonnets in circular motion to cover completely. Reheat frosting as needed to keep it pourable. Let bonnets stand 10 minutes or until set.

Remove bonnets from rack with small spatula, smoothing edges of frosting. Cut tiny hole in corner of bag with green frosting. Pipe ribbon of frosting for hatband; add bow design. Make dots and flower designs on each hat as desired.

Chocolate Bunny

Makes 1 serving

4 chocolate sandwich cookies
2 T. vanilla frosting
2 jelly beans
Coconut
Decorator gel

Place 1 cookie on flat surface to form base; make a slight indentation in center of base. Make a semicircle cut in another cookie; stand on edge, cut-side up, in indentation on base, securing with frosting.

Place 1 cookie in semicircle for head, securing with frosting. Cut remaining cookie in half for ears. Cut point off of one end of each half; secure cut end with frosting to head for ears.

Place jelly beans on base for feet. Decorate ears with coconut and face and body with gel. Store in airtight container.

★ Cocoa-Coconut Oatmeal Nests ★

Makes 48 cookies

3/4 C. butter or margarine,
   softened
3/4 C. sugar
3/4 C. brown sugar
2 eggs
1 tsp. vanilla
2 C. all-purpose flour
1/4 C. unsweetened cocoa
1 tsp. baking soda
1/2 tsp. salt
1 C. coconut
1 1/2 C. old-fashioned
   or quick oats
Candy-coated milk
   chocolate eggs

Preheat the oven to 350°F.

In a large bowl, beat butter, sugar and brown sugar until well blended; beat in eggs and vanilla. Stir together flour, cocoa, baking soda and salt; add to butter mixture, beating until blended. Stir in coconut and oats; drop by heaping teaspoons onto ungreased cookie sheet.

Bake 8 to 10 minutes or until set. Cool slightly; remove from cookie sheet to wire rack. Press 3 chocolate eggs into the center of each cookie. Cool completely.

Easter Basket Cupcakes

Makes 24 cupcakes

24 paper baking cups
1 pkg. white cake mix
1 (16 oz.) tub vanilla frosting
Flaked coconut
Green food color
Tiny jelly beans
Licorice twists

Prepare and bake cake mix according to package directions for cupcakes. Cool completely.

Frost cupcakes; set aside.

Tint coconut green by mixing with food color. Make a coconut nest on top of each cupcake. Fill coconut nests with tiny jelly beans. For basket handles, with a knife, cut licorice twists in half lengthwise; cut halves into 6" pieces. Attach basket handles by inserting ends of licorice into cupcakes.

Jelly Bean Bites

Makes 24 cookies

1 C. butter or margarine,
   softened
1/2 C. sugar
2 T. water
1 tsp. vanilla
1 egg yolk
2 1/2 C. flour
1/2 tsp. baking soda
1 bag jelly beans

Cream butter and sugar with mixer until thoroughly combined. Add water, vanilla and egg yolk and mix thoroughly. Add dry ingredients. Dough should be firm.

Refrigerate for 30 minutes.

Preheat the oven to 350°F. Roll dough into balls and place onto parchment paper-lined sheet pans. Bake for 5 minutes.

Remove from oven and make indentation on top of each cookie with thumb or spoon. Add 3 jelly beans into the indentation of each cookie, return to oven for 8 to 10 minutes or until set and light brown.

Bunnies

Makes 8 servings

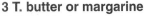

3 T. butter or margarine
1 (10 oz.) pkg. marshmallows or
**   4 C. miniature marshmallows**
6 C. crispy rice cereal or chocolate-
**   flavored crispy rice cereal**
Vanilla frosting
Red string licorice
Black string licorice
16 blue mini M&M's
8 mini marshmallows

In a large microwave safe bowl, heat margarine and marshmallows on high for 2 to 3 minutes, stirring at the halfway point. Stir until smooth.

Stir in crispy rice cereal until well coated. Allow mixture to cool slightly. Divide mixture into 3/4 cup portions. Using buttered hands shape each 3/4 cup portion of the cereal mixture into one 3-inch ball and one 2-inch ball.

Use frosting to attach the 2-inch and 3-inch balls together to form bunny body and head. Cut 16 bunny ears out of pink construction paper. Then use frosting to attach the paper bunny ears and black licorice whiskers. Make eyes with mini M&M's, mouth with red string licorice and tail with mini marshmallow, attaching with the frosting.

Noodle Nests

Makes 30 servings

30 paper baking cups
3 T. butter or margarine
3 T. creamy peanut butter
3 C. mini marshmallows
1 (12 oz.) bag chow mein
noodles
90 peanut M&M's or
jelly beans
30 marshmallow chicks

Melt margarine over low heat. Gradually stir in peanut butter, then slowly add marshmallows. Stir until mixture is melted and smooth.

Remove mixture from heat. Add noodles and stir until noodles are coated.

Spoon mixture into paper lined muffin tins.

Use back of spoon (coated in butter) to shape nests.

When nests are cool, place 3 M&M's or jelly beans and 1 marshmallow chick in each nest.

Easter Eggs

Makes 18 servings

3 T. butter or margarine
1 (10 oz.) pkg. marshmallows or
**   4 C. miniature marshmallows**
6 C. crispy rice cereal or chocolate-
**   flavored crispy rice cereal**
Piped frosting, sprinkles,
**   or small candies**

In a microwave safe bowl, heat butter and marshmallows on high for 2 to 3 minutes, stirring at the halfway point. Stir until smooth.

Add crispy rice cereal. Stir until well coated.

Divide mixture into 1/3 cup portions and shape portions into egg shapes. Decorate as desired with piped frosting, sprinkles, or small candies.

May Day Baskets

Makes 24 cupcakes

24 paper baking cups
1 pkg. yellow cake mix
1 (16 oz.) tub frosting,
  any flavor
Red or black string licorice
Mike-N-Ikes, Hot Tamales,
  Lemonheads, Sprees,
  Sweetarts and other
  candy of your choice

Prepare and bake cake mix according to package directions for cupcakes. Cool 10 minutes; remove from pan. Cool completely, about 1 hour.

Frost with frosting. Use licorice for handle. Arrange assorted candies to resemble a flower.

Mini Cupcake Mortarboards

Make 60 servings

60 mini paper baking cups
1 pkg. cake mix, any flavor
1 (16 oz.) tub vanilla frosting
60 square shortbread cookies
60 M&M's
Red or black string licorice

Prepare cake mix according to package directions for cupcakes. Place mini paper baking cups in each of 24 mini muffin cups. Fill cups 2/3 full of batter. Refrigerate remaining batter.

Bake 15 to 20 minutes or until toothpick inserted in center comes out clean; cool. Repeat with remaining batter. Leave paper baking cups on cupcakes so mortarboards are quicker and easier to make and more portable to serve.

Make tassels by cutting several pieces of string licorice into 2 1/2" lengths. Tint frosting with food color to match paper baking cups. Frost one side of cookies. Place 1 M&M on center of each. For each mortarboard, place small dollop of frosting on bottom of cupcake; top with cookie, frosting side up. Press 3 or 4 pieces of licorice into frosted cookie next to M&M. Store loosely covered.

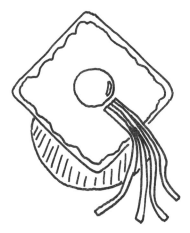

Butterfly Bites

Makes 6 servings

2 stalks of celery
12 large twist pretzels
6 T. peanut butter or cream cheese
18 raisins or currants
12 slivered almonds

Wash the celery and cut into thirds. Fill each celery stalk with 1 tablespoon of either peanut butter or cream cheese.

For the wings, gently push 2 pretzels into the filling, next to each side and connecting in the middle, running parallel to the length of the celery stick.

Arrange the raisins or currants as eyes, nose and mouth.

For antennae, push the slivered almonds into filling.

15

Easy Sugar Cookies

Make with refrigerated sugar cookie dough.

Bunny

Use 4 slices.

Slightly overlap 2 slices to form head and body.

Cut remaining slices in half.

Place 2 halves, curved sides down, angled up and just underneath lower body for feet.

Shape 2 halves into "petal" shapes; place just touching head for ears.

Bake as directed.

Bunny Face

Use 2 slices.

Use 1 slice for head, cut remaining slice in half.

Shape halves into "petal" shapes; place just touching head for ears.

Bake as directed.

Brownie Cones

Makes 12 servings

1 pkg. brownie mix
24 ice cream cups
1 (16 oz.) tub frosting,
   any flavor
Colored sprinkles or
   candies, optional

Prepare brownie mix batter as directed on package. Fill ice cream cups halfway with batter. Place cups on a cookie sheet.

Bake 25 to 30 minutes or until toothpick inserted in center comes out clean. Cool completely.

Frost brownie cones with frosting. Decorate with colored sprinkles or candies if desired.

Watermelon Cookies

Makes 36 servings

2 C. all-purpose flour
1 1/2 tsp. baking powder
1/2 tsp. salt
1/3 C. butter
1/2 C. shortening
3/4 C. sugar
1 egg
1 T. milk
1 tsp. vanilla
3 drops red food coloring
1/3 C. mini semi-sweet
 chocolate chips
1 1/2 C. powdered sugar
2 T. water
3 drops green food coloring

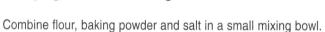

Combine flour, baking powder and salt in a small mixing bowl.

Beat butter and shortening with an electric mixer at medium speed until fluffy; gradually add sugar, beating well. Stir in egg, milk and vanilla. Gradually add flour mixture to creamed mixture, mixing well. Add a small amount of red food coloring to color dough as desired, beating until blended. Shape dough into a ball; cover and chill at least 3 hours.

Preheat the oven to 375°F.

Divide dough in half; put one portion back in refrigerator. Roll remaining portion to 1/4" thickness on a lightly floured surface. Cut dough with a 3" round cookie cutter; cut circle in half. Place on an ungreased cookie sheet. Press several mini chocolate chips in each cookie to resemble seeds. Repeat with remaining dough.

Bake 8 to 10 minutes (do not brown). Cool on wire racks.

To make frosting, combine powdered sugar and water, mixing until smooth. Add a small amount of green food coloring, mixing until blended. Dip round edge of each cookie in green frosting and place cookie on wax paper until frosting is firm.

Ants on a Log

Makes 20 servings

8 celery stalks, cut into 3 to 4" pieces
1 C. peanut butter
1/2 cup raisins

Fill celery "logs" with peanut butter.

Place raisins on peanut butter to resemble ants.

Pretzel Sparklers

Makes 24 servings

24 long rod pretzels
2 C. white chocolate, melted
1 C. sprinkles (red, white and blue),
star cake decorations or mini M&M's

Dip the pretzel rod halfway into the melted white chocolate then sprinkle the sprinkles, cake decorations or mini M&M's over the wet chocolate. Lay on wax paper or place in a cup to dry.

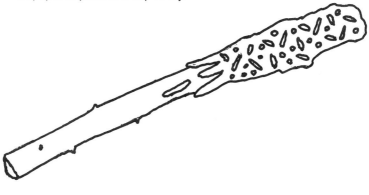

Kite Cookies

Makes 24 cookies

1 (18 oz.) pkg. refrigerated sugar cookie dough
1 (16 oz.) tub vanilla frosting
Food coloring, several colors
Fruit rollups
Red or black string licorice

Preheat the oven to 350°F.

Press cookie dough in bottom of a foil-lined 9 x 13 x 2 inch pan. Bake 11 to 15 minutes until lightly browned and done in center. Cool in pan on wire rack.

Use foil to lift cookies from pan to cutting board. Cut cookies diagonally in diamond pattern.

Tint frosting with food coloring. Frost and decorate as desired. Cut fruit rollups for bows to place at the bottom of the kite. Use licorice for kite strings. Let dry.

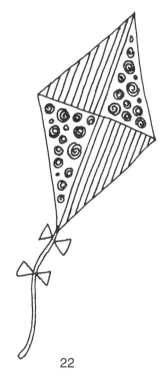

Honey Bee Pudding Cups

Makes 6 servings

6 (6 to 8 oz.) clear plastic cups
1 (4 serving size) pkg. vanilla
    instant pudding and pie filling
1 qt. (4 C.) cold milk, divided
1/4 C. honey
1 (4 serving size) pkg. chocolate
    instant pudding and pie filling
12 Stella D'Oro angel wings cookies
6 large black gum drops
Black string licorice

Pour 2 cups of the milk into a medium bowl. Add vanilla pudding mix. Beat with wire whisk for 2 minutes. Blend in honey. Let stand 5 minutes.

Pour remaining 2 cups milk into another medium bowl. Add chocolate pudding mix. Beat with wire whisk for 2 minutes. Let stand 5 minutes.

Spoon thin layers of chocolate and vanilla puddings alternately into 6 clear plastic cups, ending with chocolate pudding. Refrigerate for at least 30 minutes.

When ready to serve, decorate top of each cup to look like bees, using 2 cookies for wings and 1 gum drop for head. Cut two short pieces of black licorice for each cup and push into gum drop for antennae.

Sand Cups

Makes 8 to 10 servings

1 (12 oz.) pkg. vanilla wafers
2 C. cold milk
1 (4 serving size) pkg. vanilla
  instant pudding and pie filling
1 (8 oz.) tub whipped topping
8 to 10 (7 oz.) paper or plastic cups
Suggested garnishes: gummy
  worms or other gummy candy,
  candy flowers, "rocks",
  chopped peanuts, granola
Cocktail umbrellas, optional

Crush cookies in resealable plastic bag with rolling pin or in food processor container.

Pour cold milk into a large bowl. Add pudding mix. Beat with wire whisk for 2 minutes or until well blended. Let stand 5 minutes. Gently stir in whipped topping and 1/2 of the crushed wafers.

Place about 1 tablespoon crushed wafers in each cup. Fill cups about 3/4 full with pudding mixture. Top with remaining crushed wafers. Refrigerate 1 hour or until ready to serve. Garnish just before serving.

Bumblebee Cookies

Makes 48 cookies

1/2 C. peanut butter
1/2 C. shortening
1/3 C. brown sugar
1/3 C. honey
1 egg
1 3/4 C. all-purpose flour
3/4 tsp. baking soda
1/2 tsp. baking powder
96 small pretzel twists
96 small pretzel sticks

In a large bowl, beat peanut butter, shortening, brown sugar, honey and egg with electric mixer on medium speed or mix with a spoon. Stir in flour, baking soda and baking powder. Cover dough with plastic wrap and refrigerate about 2 hours or until firm.

Preheat the oven to 350°F. Shape dough into 1-inch balls (dough will be slightly sticky). For each cookie place 2 pretzel twists side by side with the bottoms touching on ungreased cookie sheet (the bottom is the rounded point, similar to the bottom of a heart shape). Place 1 ball of dough on center; flatten slightly. Break 2 pretzel sticks in half. Gently press 3 pretzel stick halves into dough for stripes on bee. Break fourth pretzel piece in half. Poke pieces into 1 end of dough for antennae. Repeat with remaining dough and pretzels.

Bake 11 to 13 minutes or until light golden brown. Remove from cookie sheet to wire rack; cool completely.

Dirt Cups

Makes 8 servings

8 (6 oz.) clear plastic cups
1 (4 serving size) pkg. vanilla
instant pudding and pie filling
1 (4 serving size) pkg. chocolate
instant pudding and pie filling
1 qt. (4 C.) cold milk, divided
1 C. whipped topping, divided
20 chocolate sandwich cookies,
finely crushed
16 gummy worms

Prepare vanilla and chocolate pudding mixes separately with milk as directed on packages. Let stand 5 minutes. Gently stir 1/2 cup of the whipped topping into each bowl of pudding.

Sprinkle 1 tablespoon of the cookie crumbs into bottom of each of 8 clear plastic cups; top with 1/4 cup of the vanilla pudding, 1 tablespoon of the cookie crumbs and 1/4 cup of the chocolate pudding. Sprinkle evenly with remaining cookie crumbs. Refrigerate for at least 1 hour or until ready to serve.

Garnish each serving with 2 gummy worms just before serving.

Crispy Flowers

Makes 12 servings

3 T. butter or margarine
1 (10 oz.) pkg. marshmallows or
   4 C. miniature marshmallows
6 C. crispy rice cereal
Tubes of frosting, any variety of colors

In a large microwave safe bowl, heat butter and marshmallows on high for 2 to 3 minutes, stirring at the halfway point. Stir until smooth.

Stir in crispy rice cereal until well coated. Using spatula sprayed with cooking spray or wax paper, press mixture into a 15 x 10 x 1 inch pan coated with cooking spray.

Allow mixture to cool slightly. Using flower shaped cookie cutter, cut cereal mixture into flower shapes. Decorate with frosting as desired.

Snakes

Makes 8 servings

3 T. butter or margarine
1 (10 oz.) pkg. marshmallows or
4 C. miniature marshmallows
6 C. crispy rice cereal
Cereal, licorice, berries, fruit
snacks or candies, optional
Peanut butter or frosting

In a large microwave safe bowl, heat butter and marshmallows on high for 2 to 3 minutes, stirring at the halfway point. Stir until smooth.

Stir in crispy rice cereal until well coated. When slightly cooled, shape cereal mixture into snakes using buttered hands. Place on wax paper or a surface coated with cooking spray.

Decorate snakes with cereal, licorice, berries, fruit snack or candies. Use peanut butter or frosting to make stripes or spots and attach decorations. Store in an airtight container.

 **Fourth of July Cut-Outs**

Makes 12 servings

3 T. butter or margarine
1 (10 oz.) pkg. marshmallows or
4 C. miniature marshmallows
6 C. crispy rice cereal
Red, white and blue sprinkles
12 wooden sticks, optional

In a large microwave safe bowl, heat butter and marshmallows on high for 2 to 3 minutes, stirring at the halfway point. Stir until smooth.

Stir in crispy rice cereal until well coated.

Press mixture evenly into a 15 x 10 x 1 inch pan coated with cooking spray. While warm, decorate with individual red, white and blue candy sprinkles, alternately making stripes (1/2" apart) across the top. Cool completely.

Using a star shaped cookie cutter, cut into shapes and serve on a wooden stick if desired.

Star Spangled Crispies

**1 (12 oz.) bag white
chocolate chips
4 T. butter or margarine,
melted
4 C. crispy rice cereal
1 bag M&M's or mini M&M's
with red and blue candies
separated out**

Place white chocolate chips and butter in a microwave safe bowl.

Heat on medium power for about 1 minute. Check and stir every 20 seconds so that chocolate doesn't burn.

Stir until mixture is smooth; combine with cereal and M&M's.

Drop by tablespoonfuls onto wax paper lined sheet pan to set. Store in an airtight container.

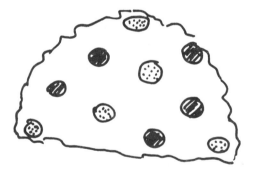

Bird's Nest Cookies

Makes 36 cookies

1 1/3 C. flaked coconut
1 C. butter or margarine,
    softened
1/3 C. sugar
1 egg
1/2 tsp. vanilla
2 C. all-purpose flour
3/4 tsp. salt
1 3/4 C. M&M's, any variety

Preheat the oven to 300°F. Spread coconut on an ungreased cookie sheet. Toast in oven, stirring occasionally, until light golden, about 25 minutes.

Remove coconut from cookie sheet and set aside.

Increase oven temperature to 350°F. In a large bowl, add butter and sugar and whip until light and fluffy; beat in egg and vanilla.

In a medium bowl, combine flour and salt. Blend into creamed mixture.

Form dough into 1 1/4-inch balls. Roll heavily into toasted coconut.

Place coconut cookies 2 inches apart on lightly greased cookie sheets. Make indentation with thumb in center of each cookie. Bake 12 to 14 minutes or until golden brown.

Remove cookies and cool completely. Fill indentation with M&M's.

Night Crawlers

Makes 6 servings

18 Starbursts
6 apples
12 fun-size Twix candy bars
1 bag fun-size Snickers candy bars
1 bag Dove Promises, milk or
**   dark chocolate**
3 T. corn syrup
1/4 C. water
6 wooden sticks
6 paper baking cups

To make 6 worms:
Unwrap 18 Starbursts. On a microwave safe dish, arrange the Starbursts in 6 lines of 3. Microwave on medium power for 30 seconds, or until the candy softens, checking every 10 seconds, being very careful not to burn. In the palm of your hands, roll each line of candy into the shape of a worm. Set aside.

To make the apples:
Press the wooden sticks vertically into the core of each apple. Lay the paper liners flat on a baking sheet and fill the bottoms evenly with chopped Twix bars. Set aside.

In a mixing bowl combine the Snickers bars, Dove Promises, corn syrup and water. Place the mixing bowl over a pot of simmering water. Stir the mixture as it melts. When mixture is shiny and smooth, turn off the heat.

One at a time, dip the apples into the chocolate mixture, rolling it so that it is completely coated. Use a table knife if necessary to aid you in covering the apple. Set each dipped apple into the paper liner filled with Twix bars.

Let cool and allow the chocolate to harden. Curl the worms around the wooden stick and apples.

Rainbow Cupcakes

Makes 24 cupcakes

24 paper baking cups
2 1/4 C. all-purpose flour
1 T. baking powder
1/2 tsp. salt
1 2/3 C. sugar
1/2 C. butter or margarine,
   softened
1 C. milk
2 tsp. vanilla
3 egg whites
Blue and assorted food colorings
1 (16 oz.) tub vanilla frosting
1 1/2 C. M&M's

Preheat the oven to 350°F.

Line 24 muffin cups with paper baking cups; set aside.

In a large bowl, combine flour, baking powder and salt. Blend in sugar, butter, milk and vanilla; beat for 2 minutes. Add egg whites; beat for 2 minutes.

Divide batter evenly among prepared muffin cups. Place 2 drops desired food coloring into each muffin cup. Swirl gently with knife.

Sprinkle evenly with 3/4 cup M&M's. Bake 20 to 25 minutes or until toothpick inserted in centers comes out clean. Cool completely on wire racks.

Combine frosting and blue food coloring. Spread frosting over cupcakes; decorate with remaining 3/4 cup M&M's to make rainbows.

Goin' Fishin' Cupcakes

Makes 24 cupcakes

24 paper baking cups
1 pkg. devil's food cake mix
1 (16 oz.) tub vanilla or
**   butter cream frosting**
Blue food coloring
24 cocktail straws
24 pieces dental floss
24 chewy fruit snacks in
**   fish or shark shapes**

Prepare and bake cake mix according to package directions for cupcakes. Cool completely.

Mix frosting and 2 or 3 drops food coloring. Frost cupcakes with blue frosting; pull up on frosting, to create "waves".

Cut each straw to make one 3" piece. Cut dental floss into 3 1/2" lengths. Attach piece of dental floss to end of each straw, using needle, to resemble fish line. Attach 1 fruit snack to end of each piece of dental floss.

Place one fishing pole on top of each cupcake with the fish "swimming" in the water.

Baseball Cookies

Makes 60 cookies

**1 (12 oz.) box wafer cookies,
crushed
1/2 C. chopped walnuts
1 (14 oz.) can sweetened
condensed milk
2 (1 oz.) squares unsweetened
chocolate, melted
Red string licorice
1 lb. white chocolate candy coating**

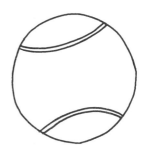

Line a work surface with wax paper. In a large bowl, mix together the condensed milk, crushed cookies, walnuts and unsweetened chocolate.

Take a tablespoonful of dough and roll into a ball. Place on wax paper and flatten gently. Repeat with the remaining dough, placing the cookies 1" apart.

Cut the licorice into 1 1/2" pieces and set aside.

Melt the white chocolate candy coating until smooth over a double boiler or in a microwave, stirring frequently. Dip the cookies into the chocolate using a fork and quickly, before the chocolate dries, place 2 licorice pieces on the cookies to form the baseball threads. If the melted chocolate starts to harden, simply reheat for a few seconds and continue dipping.

Let dry thoroughly before storing in an airtight container.

Ocean Cups

Makes 4 servings

4 clear plastic cups
**1 (4 serving size) box blue gelatin,
   prepared**
12 gummy sharks or gummy fish
4 vanilla wafers
1 small tub whipped topping
4 cocktail umbrellas, optional

Fill the plastic cups with gelatin. Place gummy sharks or fish in the gelatin. Place the cups in the refrigerator to set.

When the gelatin has set, crush the vanilla wafers very fine and cover half of the gelatin top to represent the sand of a beach.

Add a spoonful of whipped topping on the other half to represent the white caps of the ocean.

If desired, garnish each ocean cup with a cocktail umbrella.

Ice Cream Cone Cakes

Makes 24 servings

24 paper baking cups
1 pkg. cake mix, any flavor
24 flat bottom ice cream cones
1 (16 oz.) tub frosting, any flavor
Sprinkles or candies, optional

Place paper baking cup in each of 24 muffin cups.

Prepare cake mix as directed on package except fill each cup 2/3 full of batter. Place ice cream cone upside down on batter in each cup.

Bake 20 minutes (cones may tilt on batter); cool completely. Remove paper baking cups. Frost cake with frosting, and decorate with sprinkles or candies as desired.

Crispy Berry Skewers

Makes 16 servings

3 T. butter or margarine
1 (10 oz.) pkg. marshmallows or
**   4 C. miniature marshmallows**
6 C. crispy rice cereal
16 (12") skewers
32 marshmallows
32 fresh strawberries

In a large microwave safe bowl, heat butter and marshmallows on high for 2 to 3 minutes, stirring at the halfway point. Stir until smooth.

Stir in crispy rice cereal until well coated.

Press mixture evenly into a 9 x 13 x 2 inch pan coated with cooking spray. Let cool. Cut cereal mixture into 1 x 1-inch squares.

On each 12-inch skewer, alternately thread a crispy square, marshmallow, strawberry, square, strawberry, marshmallow and end with a square.

Fall

Scarecrow Cupcakes

Make 16 cupcakes

16 paper baking cups
1 1/2 C. biscuit and baking mix
1/2 C. sugar
1/2 C. milk
2 T. shortening
1 T. vanilla
1 egg
1 (16 oz.) tub vanilla or
  butter cream frosting
8 fudge-dipped flat-bottom
  ice cream cones
Strawberry chewy fruit snack rolls
Shredded whole wheat
  cereal biscuits,
  crushed or coconut
Assorted candies, such as candy corn,
  red string licorice and small gumdrops
32 candy eyes

Preheat the oven to 375°F. Place paper baking cup in each of 16 muffin cups.

In a large bowl, beat biscuit and baking mix, sugar, milk, shortening, vanilla and egg on low speed for 30 seconds, scraping bowl occasionally. Fill muffin cups about half full.

Bake 15 to 20 minutes or until toothpick inserted in center comes out clean. Immediately remove from pan; cool completely.

Frost cupcakes with vanilla frosting. Decorate each ice cream cone with a bow made with fruit rolls. Place ice cream cone upside down on each cupcake for hat. Arrange crushed cereal or coconut on cupcakes for hair. Use candy corn for nose (lay flat, small tip towards the top), red licorice and small gumdrops for mouth and candy eyes for eyes.

Spider Cupcakes

Make 16 cupcakes

16 paper baking cups
1 1/2 C. biscuit and baking mix
1/2 C. sugar
1/2 C. milk
2 T. shortening
1 T. vanilla
1 egg
32 candy eyes
1 (16 oz.) tub chocolate frosting
48 large black gumdrops
Black string licorice,
    cut into 4-inch pieces

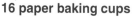

Preheat the oven to 375°F. Place paper baking cup in each of 16 muffin cups.

In a large bowl, beat biscuit and baking mix, sugar, milk, shortening, vanilla and egg on low speed for 30 seconds, scraping bowl occasionally. Fill muffin cups about half full.

Bake 15 to 20 minutes or until toothpick inserted in center comes out clean. Immediately remove from pan; cool completely.

Frost cupcakes with chocolate frosting. Squeeze large black gumdrops, one at a time, through garlic press to form hair; arrange on cupcakes. Insert black licorice pieces into cupcakes for legs. Place a large black gumdrop on cupcake for the spider's head. Secure candy eyes on gumdrop with frosting.

Witchfinger Cookies

Makes 48 cookies

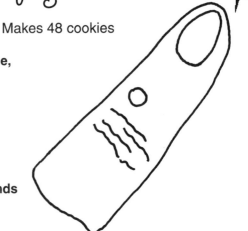

**1 C. butter or margarine,
  softened
1 C. powdered sugar
1 egg
2 tsp. almond extract
2 3/4 C. flour
1 tsp. baking powder
1 tsp. salt
Whole blanched almonds
Green food color
Raspberry jam**

Mix together butter, powdered sugar, egg and extract. Add flour, baking powder and salt, plus a little green food coloring to create a ghoulish look. Form into a soft dough. Refrigerate for 30 minutes.

Preheat the oven to 375°F. Take a tablespoon of dough and roll out into a long finger shape. Dip an almond into a little jam and then press into the end for the fingernail. Make a knuckle shape in the center, slash in a few wrinkles and top with small bits of dough to make some warts. Bake 20 minutes on a slightly greased cookie sheet.

Cupcake Graveyard

Makes 24 cupcakes

24 paper baking cups
1 pkg. chocolate cake mix
2 (16 oz.) tubs vanilla frosting
3/4 C. chocolate sandwich
  cookie crumbs
24 chocolate covered graham
  cracker cookies

Prepare and bake cake mix according to package directions for cupcakes. Cool completely.

In a medium bowl, mix 1 tub of frosting with the cookie crumbs. Frost cupcakes.

Fill a pastry bag fitted with a plain tip (or use a plastic baggie, cutting a tiny hole in the corner), with remaining white frosting. Write R.I.P. on each chocolate covered graham cracker cookie. Stand a decorated cookie on top of each cupcake so that it looks like a tombstone.

Place the cupcakes on a large cookie sheet that has been covered with green paper. Place paper ghosts and bats randomly throughout the graveyard.

★ Frightfully Easy Ghost Cookies ★

Makes 32 cookies

12 oz. vanilla-flavored candy
   coating, cut into pieces
1 (1 lb.) pkg. Nutter Butter cookies
64 miniature chocolate chips

In a small saucepan, melt candy coating over low heat, stirring constantly until smooth.

Line cookie sheets with wax paper. Holding cookie with tongs, dip entire top and side of each cookie into melted coating, letting excess drip off. Lay flat, coated side up, on wax paper-lined cookie sheets. Place 2 chocolate chips in coating to form eyes. Let stand about 10 minutes until set.

Yummy Mummy Cookies

Makes 30 cookies

2/3 C. butter or margarine, softened
1 C. sugar
2 tsp. vanilla extract
2 eggs
2 1/2 C. all-purpose flour
1/2 C. unsweetened cocoa
1/4 tsp. baking soda
1/2 tsp. salt
1 C. mini semi-sweet chocolate chips
1 to 2 (10 oz.) pkgs. white
   chocolate chips
1 to 2 T. shortening (do not use butter,
   margarine, spread or oil)
Additional mini semi-sweet
   chocolate chips

In a large bowl, beat butter, sugar and vanilla until creamy. Add eggs; beat well. Combine flour, cocoa, baking soda and salt; gradually add to butter mixture, beating well. Stir in 1 cup mini chocolate chips. Refrigerate dough 20 minutes or until firm enough to handle.

Preheat the oven to 350°F. For mummy body, roll 1 tablespoon dough into 3 1/2" long carrot shape; place on ungreased cookie sheet. For head, roll 1 teaspoon dough into a ball the size of a grape; press onto wide end of body. Repeat procedure with remaining dough.

Bake 8 to 9 minutes or until set. Cool slightly; remove from cookie sheet to wire rack. Cool completely.

Microwave 1 2/3 cups (10 oz.) white chips and 1 tablespoon shortening in microwave safe pie plate or shallow bowl on high for 1 minute; stir until chips are melted.

Place 1 cookie at a time on table knife or narrow metal spatula. Spoon white chip mixture over just the top of cookie to coat; place on wax paper. If mixture begins to thicken, return to microwave for a few seconds. Melt additional chips with shortening, if needed for additional coating. As coating begins to set on cookies, use toothpick to score lines in body and on face to resemble mummy. Place two mini chocolate chips on each for eyes. Store, covered, in cool dry place.

Black Cat Cupcakes

Makes 24 cupcakes

24 paper baking cups
1 bag Twix fun-size bars
1 pkg. chocolate cake mix
1 (16 oz.) tub chocolate
   frosting
1 bag Skittles fun-size
1 bag red licorice twists
1 bag Starburst Original
   Fruit Chews fun-size

Chop 12 Twix bars and set aside.

Prepare cake mix batter according to package directions.

Pour 1/8 cup of batter into each cupcake liner. Top with a generous tablespoon of chopped Twix bars and finish with a final layer of 1/4 cup of batter.

Bake for the recommended time or until a toothpick inserted in cupcake is clean when removed. Cool cupcakes completely before frosting.

Frost each cupcake and decorate using Skittles for the eyes (placed on its side for oval eyes) and nose, licorice twists cut in half lengthwise for the whiskers and Starbursts cut in half diagonally for the ears.

Edible Spiders

Makes 24 servings

1 C. semi-sweet chocolate chips
1 tsp. butter or margarine
24 large marshmallows
1 (6 oz.) pkg. chow mein noodles
1 (12 oz.) pkg. mini M&M's

Line a cookie sheet with wax paper. Stick 4 chow mein noodles into each side of marshmallow for legs and arrange on wax paper.

In a microwave safe bowl, combine chocolate chips and butter. Microwave until melted. Stir occasionally until chocolate is smooth. Pour chocolate into a resealable plastic bag.

Using scissors, cut one tiny corner off the bag of melted chocolate. Drizzle over the marshmallow spiders. Attach 2 candies to each marshmallow for eyes. Chill until chocolate hardens.

Graveyard Cups

Makes 24 servings

24 (12 oz.) clear plastic cups
2 pkgs. chocolate sandwich cookies
2 large pkgs. chocolate pudding, prepared
Whipped cream
24 Pepperidge Farms Milano cookies
Brown or black cake decorating gel
24 gummi worms

Crush all chocolate sandwich cookies in food processor. In the bottom of each cup, place about 1 tablespoon of crushed cookies.

Mix remainder of cookies in pudding mixture, holding out about 3 cups for topping. Divide pudding mixture equally into the plastic cups.

Spoon about 2 tablespoons crushed cookies over pudding. Poke 1 gummi worm down in dirt, still showing on top.

On each Milano cookie, write on top half "RIP" with cake decorating gel, and stick down in the back of the cup to resemble a tombstone.

 ★ Spooky Halloween Cookies ★

Makes 24 cookies

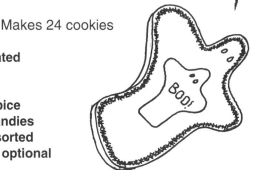

1 (18 oz.) pkg. refrigerated
   sugar cookie dough
3/4 C. all-purpose flour
1/2 tsp. pumpkin pie spice
Assorted color hard candies
Decorating gel and assorted
   color sugar crystals, optional

Preheat the oven to 350°F. Line baking sheets with aluminum foil. Knead flour and pumpkin pie spice into cookie dough until smooth. Roll dough to a 1/4" thickness.

Using large cookie cutters, cut dough into desired shapes; transfer to prepared baking sheets. Using small cookie cutters, cut out centers. Reroll scraps for additional cookies.

Bake 10 to 12 minutes or until lightly browned. Put the baking sheets on a wire rack to cool.

Place each color candy in separate resealable plastic bags; seal bags. Using a meat mallet or rolling pin, break candies into small pieces.

Spoon candy pieces into center of cookie cutouts, filling the space completely. Brush off any candy crumbs from the cookie surface.

Return cookies to the oven. Bake until candy pieces are just melted and smooth, about 2 minutes. Transfer to wire racks and cool completely. Peel cookies from foil; set cookies aside.

If desired, decorate cookies with decorating gel and sugar crystals.

Creepy Crawly Spiders

Makes 24 servings

2 C. miniature marshmallows
1 pkg. semi-sweet baking
** chocolate, melted**
Black or red string licorice
Assorted candies

Mix marshmallows and melted chocolate until marshmallows are completely coated. Drop by spoonfuls onto wax paper to make 24 clusters.

Decorate each with 8 short pieces of licorice for legs and assorted candies for eyes. Let stand at room temperature or refrigerate until firm.

Store in airtight container in cool location.

Witches' Hats

Makes 32 cookies

32 milk chocolate Kisses
1 (11 1/2 oz.) pkg. fudge-
   striped shortbread cookies
1 tube orange or red
   decorating icing

Pipe decorating icing on the bottom of a chocolate Kiss around the edge. Place chocolate Kiss on the chocolate bottom of each cookie, covering the hole in the cookie.

Pipe decorating icing around base of chocolate kiss and decorate with a icing bow.

Witches' Brooms

Makes 20 cookies

1/2 C. brown sugar
1/2 C. butter or margarine,
** softened**
2 T. water
1 tsp. vanilla
1 1/2 C. all-purpose flour
1/8 tsp. salt
10 pretzel rods, about 8 1/2" long,
** cut crosswise in half**
2 tsp. shortening
2/3 C. semi-sweet chocolate chips
Butterscotch-flavored chips,
** melted**

Preheat the oven to 350°F. In a medium bowl, mix brown sugar, butter, water and vanilla. Stir in flour and salt. Shape dough into twenty 1 1/4" balls.

Place pretzel rod halves on ungreased cookie sheet. Press dough ball onto cut end of each pretzel rod. Press dough with fork to resemble "bristles" of broom.

Bake about 12 minutes or until set, but not brown. Remove from cookie sheet. Cool completely on wire rack for about 30 minutes.

Cover cookie sheet with wax paper. Place brooms on wax paper. Heat shortening and chocolate chips over low heat or in microwave, stirring occasionally, until melted and smooth. Spoon melted chocolate over the base of the brooms covering about 1 inch of the pretzel handle and the top part of cookie bristles. Drizzle melted butterscotch chips over the chocolate broom base. Let stand until set.

Black Cat Cookies

Makes 54 cookies

1 C. crunchy peanut butter
2 eggs
1/3 C. water
1 pkg. chocolate cake mix
M&M's (plain)
Red cinnamon candies

Preheat the oven to 375°F. In a medium bowl, beat together peanut butter, eggs and water. Gradually add cake mix. Mix well. Form dough into 1-inch balls.

Place on ungreased cookie sheet. Flatten balls with bottom of glass dipped in sugar. Pinch out 2 ears at top of cookie. Add M&M's for eyes and red cinnamon candy for a nose. Press fork into dough to form whiskers. Bake for 8 to 10 minutes.

Chocolate Mice

Makes 12 servings

**4 (1 oz.) squares semi-sweet
chocolate**
1/3 C. sour cream
**1 C. finely crushed chocolate
wafer cookies**
**1/3 C. finely crushed chocolate
wafer cookies**
1/3 C. powdered sugar
24 silver dragees decorating candy
1/4 C. sliced almonds
12 pcs. red string licorice

Melt the chocolate and combine with sour cream. Stir in 1 cup crushed
chocolate wafer cookies and mix well. Cover and refrigerate until firm.

Roll dough by level tablespoonfuls into balls. Mold to a slight point at one
end (the nose).

Roll dough balls in powdered sugar (for white mice) or in crushed chocolate
wafer cookies (for dark mice). On each mouse, place 2 dragees for eyes,
2 almond slices for ears and a licorice string for the tail.

Refrigerate for at least 2 hours until firm.

⋆ Scary Spiderweb Cupcakes ⋆

Makes 24 cupcakes

24 paper baking cups
1 pkg. devil's food cake mix
Red and yellow food coloring
1 (16 oz.) tub vanilla frosting
1 tube black decorating gel
48 black licorice gumdrops

Prepare and bake cake mix according to package directions for cupcakes. Cool completely.

Make orange frosting by stirring a few drops red and yellow food colors into frosting; frost cupcakes.

Draw 3 or 4 circles of black decorating gel on each cupcake, one inside the other. Pull knife from the center outward around the cupcake to make a web. Use 2 gumdrops for each cupcake to make a spider. Roll out 1 gumdrop and cut out 8 strips for legs; place other gumdrop on top of cupcake. Add gumdrop strips for legs. Store loosely covered.

Ghostly Snacks

Makes 12 servings

3 T. butter or margarine
1 (10 oz.) pkg. regular
   marshmallows or 4 C.
   miniature marshmallows
6 C. crispy rice cereal
12 wooden sticks
Flaked coconut
Decorating gel

In a microwave safe bowl, heat butter and marshmallows on high for 2 to 3 minutes, stirring at the halfway point. Stir until smooth.

Add crispy rice cereal. Stir until well coated.

Divide warm cereal mixture into 1/2 cup portions. Using buttered hands, shape into ghosts and insert wooden sticks.

Coat with flaked coconut and create eyes and mouth with decorating gel. Cool completely and wrap individually in plastic wrap.

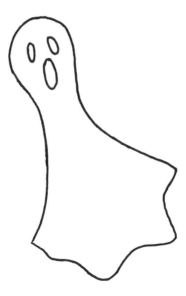

Halloween Cats

Makes 12 servings

3 T. butter or margarine
1 (10 oz.) pkg. regular
marshmallows or
4 C. miniature
marshmallows
6 C. chocolate flavored
crispy rice cereal
Candy corn
Skittles
Black string licorice

In a microwave safe bowl, heat butter and marshmallows on high for 2 to 3 minutes, stirring at the halfway point. Stir until smooth.

Add crispy rice cereal. Stir until well coated.

Divide warm cereal mixture into 1/2 cup portions. Using buttered hands, shape into a ball.

Create ears with candy corn, eyes with Skittles (placed on its side for oval eyes), nose with a Skittle and whiskers with black string licorice.

Halloween Popcorn Hands

Clear plastic kitchen gloves
Candy corn
Popped popcorn
Orange yarn
Spider rings

Place a piece of candy corn in each glove finger to resemble fingernails. Fill the rest of the glove with popcorn and then tie the glove off at the wrist with orange yarn. Put spider ring on a glove finger.

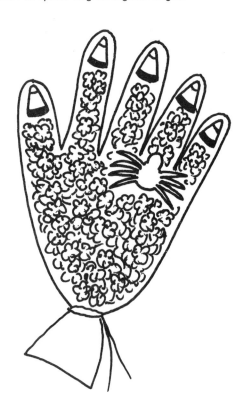

58

Spooky Spider Cupcakes

Makes 24 cupcakes

24 paper baking cups
1 pkg. chocolate cake mix
1 (1 lb.) pkg. black string licorice
1 (16 oz.) tub white frosting
48 pieces candy corn
48 red cinnamon candies
1/4 C. orange decorator sugar

Prepare and bake cake mix according to package directions for cupcakes. Cool completely.

Cut licorice into 3" long pieces. Working with one or two cupcakes at a time, so the frosting doesn't set before decorating, frost the cupcakes with the white frosting. Insert licorice pieces into the outer edges of the cupcakes to make the legs of the spider, 3 or 4 legs on each side. Place 2 pieces of candy corn on the front of the cupcake for fangs and use 2 red cinnamon candies as eyes. Sprinkle with decorator sugar. Repeat with remaining cupcakes.

Owl Cookies

Makes 72 cookies

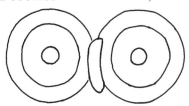

1 1/4 C. M&M's, divided
2 T. milk
1 (24 oz.) pkg. dry sugar
   cookie mix
1 C. cashew halves

In a small saucepan combine 3/4 cup M&M's and milk. Melt over low heat stirring until smooth. Remove from heat.

Prepare cookie mix according to package directions. Stir melted chocolate into half the dough. Form chocolate dough into two 12" long rolls about 1" in diameter. Wrap in wax paper or foil. Chill until firm, about 2 hours.

Divide plain dough in half. On a well-floured surface, roll each plain half out to a 12 x 6" rectangle. Place a chocolate roll on long edge. Roll up, pressing dough lightly together so plain dough encases chocolate roll. Repeat with remaining dough.

Wrap each roll in wax paper or foil. Chill until firm, about 2 hours. Preheat the oven to 375°F.

Cut each roll into 1/4" slices. Place 2 slices so they are touching on greased baking sheet. In the center of each chocolate circle, place one of the remaining M&M's for eyes. Where the slices touch, place a cashew to form nose.

Bake 8 to 10 minutes or until the plain cookie is lightly browned. Cool cookies on baking sheets for 2 to 3 minutes. Remove and cool on wire racks.

Chocolate Mini Footballs

Makes 12 servings

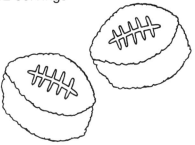

3 T. butter or margarine
1 (10 oz.) pkg. regular
  marshmallows or 4 C.
  miniature marshmallows
1/2 C. peanut butter
6 C. chocolate flavored
  crispy rice cereal
1 (16 oz.) tub vanilla frosting

In a microwave safe bowl, heat butter and marshmallows on high for 2 to 3 minutes, stirring at the halfway point. Stir until smooth.

Mix peanut butter into the marshmallow mixture.

Add crispy rice cereal. Stir until well coated.

Shape mixture into 3-inch footballs.

Use prepared frosting to pipe on football markings and stitching. Best if served the same day.

Pumpkin Candy Packages

Makes 24 servings

24 (8 x 8") sheets of plastic wrap
12 C. assorted candy
Scissors
48 10 x 10" sheets of
   orange tissue paper
Green raffia

For each package, place one sheet of plastic wrap on work surface. Spoon 1/2 cup candy onto center of plastic wrap.

Pull plastic wrap up around candy to form a ball; twist at top to seal. Trim off excess plastic wrap with scissors.

Place candy ball in center of two squares of tissue paper. Gather edges at top of ball and twist; tie with raffia. If desired, draw on a jack-o-lantern face. Repeat with remaining materials.

Candy Corn Popcorn Balls

Makes 15 servings

1/4 C. butter or margarine
1 (10 1/2 oz.) pkg. miniature
marshmallows
1 (4-serving size) pkg. gelatin,
any flavor
12 C. popped popcorn
1 C. candy corn

In a large microwave safe bowl, microwave butter and marshmallows on high for 1 1/2 to 2 minutes or until marshmallows are puffed. Stir in gelatin until well mixed.

Pour marshmallow mixture over popcorn and candy corn in large bowl. Mix lightly until well coated. Shape into 15 balls with greased or moistened hands. Wrap each ball in plastic wrap and tie with raffia or ribbon, if desired.

Chocolatey Football Bites

Makes 18 servings

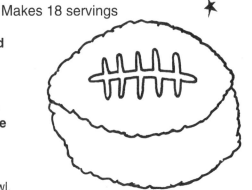

**4 C. chocolate flavored
  crispy rice cereal
6 squares semi-sweet
  baking chocolate
1/2 C. light corn syrup
1 T. butter or margarine
1/2 tsp. vanilla
White decorating gel**

Place cereal in a large bowl.

Microwave chocolate, corn syrup and butter in large microwave safe bowl on high 2 1/2 minutes, stirring after 1 1/2 minutes. Stir in vanilla.

Pour chocolate mixture over cereal and mix well. Shape into 2-inch football shapes, using slightly moistened hands. Cool completely. Use decorating gel to add lacings for footballs.

Pumpkin-Patch Cookies

Makes 36 cookies

3 1/2 C. all-purpose flour
1 tsp. baking powder
1 1/2 C. butter or margarine,
   softened
1/4 tsp. orange paste food coloring
1 C. sugar
1 egg
1 tsp. vanilla
1 C. creamy chocolate frosting
18 green jelly beans,
   cut crosswise in half

Preheat the oven to 400°F. In a medium bowl, stir together flour and baking powder. Set flour mixture aside.

In a large bowl, beat butter and food coloring with an electric mixer on medium speed for 30 seconds. Add sugar and beat until fluffy.

Add egg and vanilla, then beat well. Stir in flour mixture. Do not chill dough.

Put the flower plate onto a cookie press. Pack dough, half at a time, into the cookie press. Press dough into flowers on ungreased cookie sheets.

Bake 7 to 8 minutes or until cookies are lightly browned around the edges. Remove cookies to a wire rack and cool completely.

Spread the flat side of half of the cookies with frosting. Top with remaining cookies to form pumpkins. For stems, attach 1 jelly bean half to the top of each cookie with frosting. Let stand for 1 to 2 hours or until frosting is slightly dry.

Brownie Footballs

Makes 24 servings

1 pkg. brownie mix
   (with chocolate syrup pouch)
1 (16 oz.) tub chocolate frosting
1 C. white chocolate chips
1 T. milk
1 T. butter

Preheat the oven to 350°F. Line 13 x 9 x 2 inch pan with aluminum foil, letting foil hang 2" over short ends of pan. Prepare and bake brownie mix as directed on package, using 3 eggs for cake-like brownies. Cool completely.

Remove brownies from pan, using foil to lift. Cut brownies into football shapes, using a cookie cutter or knife. Frost footballs with frosting.

Place white chocolate chips, milk and butter in a small microwave safe bowl. Microwave uncovered on medium-high for 1 minute, stir. Microwave about 10 seconds longer or until chips are melted. Drizzle or pipe melted chips over frosting to look like football laces.

Turkey Treats

Makes 24 servings

24 chocolate sandwich cookies
24 Hershey Kisses
120 pieces candy corn
Red or orange mini M&M's
1 (16 oz.) tub chocolate frosting

Use frosting to attach Kisses base to the striped side of each cookie, close to the edge.

Use frosting to attach 5 candy corn, tips down, to each cookie above the Kiss in a fan-shape to resemble feathers.

Use frosting to attach 1 mini M&M to the top of the Kiss for the comb and 2 at the bottom for the wattle.

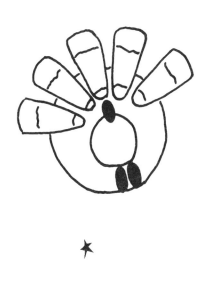

Harvest Pumpkin Tarts

Makes 24 servings

**1 (14 oz.) can sweetened
condensed milk
1 1/4 C. canned pumpkin
2 T. brown sugar
1 egg
1/4 tsp. ground cinnamon
1/4 tsp. ground nutmeg
24 (3-inch) tart shells**

Preheat the oven to 375°F.

Whisk together sweetened condensed milk, pumpkin, brown sugar, egg, cinnamon and nutmeg. Pour evenly into tart shells.

Bake 18 minutes or until center is just set and pastry is golden.

Cool and garnish as desired.

Thanksgiving Turkey Cookies

Makes 20 cookies

1 (18 oz.) pkg. refrigerated sugar
   cookie dough
Candy corn
1 (16 oz.) tub vanilla frosting
Brown, red and yellow paste or get
   icing colors (not liquid food color)

Preheat the oven to 350°F. Bake cookies as directed on package. Cool 20 minutes or until completely cooled.

Divide frosting evenly into 4 small bowls. Tint 1 bowl of frosting with brown icing color; blend well. Tint another bowl of frosting with red icing color; blend well. Tint third bowl with yellow icing color; blend well. Leave remaining bowl of frosting white.

Spoon each color of frosting into resealable plastic baggies; seal bags. Cut a tiny hole in the bottom corner of each bag.

On each cookie, attach 6 candy corn, tips down, with a small amount of white frosting for feathers. Pipe a small brown frosting circle onto each cookie to resemble a turkey face. Add eyes and beak with yellow frosting onto brown circle and use the red frosting for the wattle.

Candy Turkeys

Makes 24 servings

1 (16 oz.) pkg. fudge
striped shortbread cookies
1 (13 oz.) pkg. Rolo's,
unwrapped
1 (14 oz.) pkg. individually
wrapped caramels, unwrapped
1 (14 oz.) pkg. candy corn
1 (16 oz.) tub chocolate frosting

Stack on their sides, 1 caramel, 1 Rolo and 1 candy corn (lay flat). Use a dab of frosting to hold all together.

Place a dab of frosting on back of the caramel and attach to the bottom edge of a cookie so the cookie stands upright and the candy corn points down.

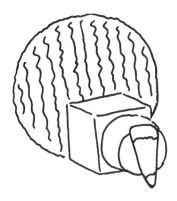

Easy Sugar Cookies

Make with refrigerated sugar cookie dough.

Witch

Use 2 slices.

Cut narrow strip from 2 sides of 1 slice to form hair and triangular hat. Roll second slice into ball to form head.

Place narrow strips, curved edges in, about 1/8" from sides of head to form hair.

Crimp triangular piece at bottom to form hat. Place hat above head, edges touching.

Bake as directed.

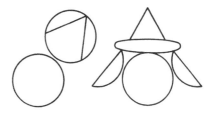

Pumpkin

Use 1 slice, 1/2" thick.

Cut a small pie-shaped wedge out of slice to form stem of pumpkin. Push dough together where wedge was removed to form whole slice.

Place wedge, pointed end out, at top of slice to form stem.

Bake as directed.

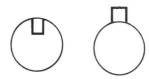

Easy Sugar Cookies

Make with refrigerated sugar cookie dough. ✦

Cat

Use 2 slices.

Cut bottom 1/3 off 1 slice. Roll remaining 2/3 slice into ball to form head.

Cut a small pie-shaped wedge out of second slice to form tail. Push dough together where wedge was removed to form whole slice for body. Place ball above slice to form head and body.

Cut 1/3 slice into 2 equal pieces. Attach pieces to head and shape to form pointed ears. Attach wedge to 1 side of body, pointed end out, to form tail.

Bake as directed.

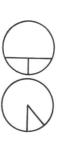 

Turkey

Roll heaping tablespoon dough into ball; flatten slightly.

Roll 3 teaspoons dough into 3 oblong balls and place 1/4" apart for feathers.

Using 1 teaspoon dough, shape 2/3 for head and 1/3 for feet.

Bake as directed.

Winter

Snowman Snacks

3 T. butter or margarine
1 (10 oz.) pkg. marshmallows or
  4 C. miniature marshmallows
6 C. crispy rice cereal or chocolate-
  flavored crispy rice cereal
Chocolate frosting
Vanilla frosting
Mini M&M's or mini chocolate chips
Fruit rollups, optional

In a microwave safe bowl, heat butter and marshmallows on high for 2 to 3 minutes, stirring at the halfway point. Stir until smooth.

Add crispy rice cereal. Stir until well coated.

Using a buttered spatula or wax paper, press mixture evenly in 15 x 10 x 1 inch pan coated with cooking spray. Using a 4" snowman cookie cutter, cut into snowman shapes when cooled. If a snowman cookie cutter is not available, use 1 1/2", 1 3/5" and 2" round cookie cutters. Using frosting, connect each circle to make a snowman.

Frost on hats using chocolate frosting. Use vanilla frosting to frost or pipe around the outer edges of the snowman. Use mini M&M's or mini chocolate chips for eyes, nose and buttons. Cut fruit rollups into short strips and use as scarves if desired.

Candy Sleighs

Makes 24 servings

24 fun-size candy bars
48 miniature candy canes
48 gummy bears
1 C. chocolate chips
Red string licorice, optional

Place chocolate chips in a microwave safe bowl. Microwave on medium in 30 second intervals, stirring between each interval, until chocolate is thoroughly melted.

Use melted chocolate to attach candy canes onto the sides of the candy bar to create a sleigh. Attach gummy bears sitting on the top of the candy bar with the melted chocolate. If desired, add a string of red licorice for a rope.

Caramel Popcorn Balls

Makes 15 servings

5 T. vegetable oil
2 1/2 C. popping corn
1/4 C. butter or margarine
1 C. brown sugar
1/2 C. corn syrup
2/3 C. sweetened condensed milk
1/2 tsp. vanilla

Add 1 tablespoon of the oil to a 4-quart covered saucepan and heat over high heat. When oil is hot, add 1/2 cup of popping corn. Keep pan moving constantly. When corn stops popping, remove from heat. Place popped corn in oven to keep warm. Repeat until all corn has been popped. Set aside.

In a medium saucepan with a candy thermometer inserted, combine butter, brown sugar and corn syrup. Stir well and bring to boiling over medium heat. Stir in condensed milk; simmer, stirring constantly, until thermometer reads 238°F. Stir in vanilla.

Pour caramel over popped corn and stir to coat. Butter hands lightly; shape into balls about 3 1/2" in diameter. Wrap in plastic wrap.

Snowmen Faces

Makes 20 cookies

1/4 C. vanilla frosting
1 (14 oz.) pkg. (20) white fudge
    covered chocolate sandwich cookies
1 T. miniature chocolate chips
10 small gumdrops
2 orange slice jelly candies,
    flattened slightly
Red decorating gel

Place frosting in small resealable plastic bag. Cut tiny hole in bottom corner of bag.

On each sandwich cookie, use small amount of frosting to attach chocolate chips for eyes. Cut each gumdrop in half; attach cut sides with frosting to sides of cookie to resemble earmuffs.

Attach small wedge cut from slightly flattened orange slice jelly candy for nose. Draw mouth with red decorating gel. Let stand about 30 minutes or until frosting is set.

Penguin Cupcakes

Makes 24 cupcakes

24 paper baking cups
1 pkg. white cake mix
2 (16 oz.) tubs vanilla frosting
36 thin chocolate cookies
  (Keebler Grasshopper
  Fudge Mint cookies or
  Girl Scout Thin Mints)
12 dried apricots
48 brown mini M&M's

Prepare and bake cake mix according to package directions for cupcakes. Cool completely.

Frost each cupcake with vanilla frosting using 1 tub. Cut cookies in half. Place 3 halves on top of each cupcake, using 1 half for the face and 2 for the wings. Cut apricots into 6 pieces, as you would cut a pie, to create triangles. Use 2 triangles for feet that point up between the wings and using extra frosting, attach 1 triangle for the beak at the base of the head. Attach 2 mini M&M's with frosting for eyes.

Snowmen Cookies

Makes 48 cookies

1 (8 oz.) pkg. cream cheese, softened
3/4 C. butter, softened
1 C. powdered sugar
1/2 tsp. vanilla
2 1/4 C. all-purpose flour
1/2 tsp. baking soda
Powdered sugar
Decorating gel
24 miniature Reese's Peanut Butter Cups

In a large bowl, beat cream cheese, butter, powdered sugar and vanilla at medium speed with electric mixer until well blended.

Add flour and soda; mix well. Refrigerate for 30 minutes.

Preheat the oven to 325°F.

For each snowman, shape dough into two small balls, one slightly larger than the other. Place balls, slightly overlapping, on ungreased cookie sheet; flatten with bottom of glass.

Bake 18 to 20 minutes or until light golden brown. Cool on wire rack.

Sprinkle each snowman with sifted powdered sugar. Decorate with icing as desired. Cut miniature peanut butter cups in half for hats and attach using decorating gel.

Cinnamon Polar Bears

Makes 48 cookies

1 C. sugar
1 C. butter or margarine,
softened
1 egg
2 1/4 C. all-purpose flour
1 tsp. cinnamon
Powdered sugar
96 miniature chocolate chips
48 red cinnamon candies

In a large bowl, combine sugar and butter; beat until light and fluffy. Add egg; beat well. Lightly spoon flour into measuring cup; level off. Add flour and cinnamon; blend well. Cover dough with plastic wrap; refrigerate for 1 hour for easier handling.

Preheat the oven to 350°F.

For each cookie, shape dough into 1-inch ball, placing 2 inches apart on ungreased cookie sheets. Flatten slightly. Shape 3 more 1/4-inch balls. Place 2 of the balls above and touching larger ball for ears and 1 ball on top to resemble snout. Flatten slightly.

Bake 11 to 15 minutes or until firm to the touch. Immediately remove from cookie sheets. Lightly sprinkle cookie with powdered sugar. Press 2 chocolate chips into each cookie for eyes and 1 cinnamon candy for nose.

Snowman Crispies

Makes 5 servings

3 T. butter or margarine
1 (10 oz.) pkg. marshmallows
6 C. crispy rice cereal
5 round red peppermint candies
8 red jelly beans
10 chocolate chips
25 miniature chocolate chips
1 fruit rollup, cut into 3/4" strips
15 red cinnamon candies
10 pretzel sticks

Line a baking sheet with wax paper and coat with nonstick cooking spray.

In a microwave safe bowl, heat butter and marshmallows on high for 2 to 3 minutes, stirring at the halfway point. Stir until smooth.

Add crispy rice cereal. Stir until well coated.

Using a 3/4 cup portion of the mixture for each, form 5 balls and place on the baking sheet. Using a 1/3 cup portion for each, form 5 more balls. Place the smaller balls on top of the larger ones, forming snowmen.

Decorate by placing 1 jelly bean on 1 peppermint candy for the hat; place on top of smaller ball. Slice a jelly bean in 1/2 lengthwise for the nose, 2 chocolate chips make the eyes and 5 mini chips make the mouth. A strip of fruit rollup adds a scarf, 3 red cinnamon candies for buttons and 2 pretzel sticks make the arms.

Gingerbread Boys and Girls

Makes 30 cookies

1/3 C. shortening
1 C. brown sugar
1 1/2 C. dark molasses
2/3 C. cold water
7 C. all-purpose flour
2 tsp. baking soda
1 tsp. salt
1 tsp. ground allspice
1 tsp. ground ginger
1 tsp. crushed cloves (optional)
1 tsp. ground cinnamon
2 egg yolks
10 drops food coloring
1/2 tsp. water
3/4 C. raisins or mini M&M's
Assorted candies for decorations

In a large bowl, mix shortening, brown sugar and molasses thoroughly. Stir in water. Blend flour, soda, salt and spices; stir into molasses mixture. Chill for about 1 hour.

Preheat the oven to 350°F. Roll the dough about 1/4" thick. Cut with boy and girl cookie cutters.

Make egg yolk paint by blending egg yolks and 1/2 teaspoon water. Divide the yolk among a few small bowls and add food coloring to each cup for desired color. Paint the clothes and decorations on the cookies as desired. Carefully transfer to a lightly greased baking sheet. Press raisins or M&M's into dough for eyes, nose and mouth. Decorate with candies as desired.

Bake 10 to 12 minutes. Cool slightly, then carefully remove from baking sheet.

Christmas Wreaths

Makes 8 servings

1/2 C. butter or margarine
1 (10 oz.) bag marshmallows
2 tsp. vanilla
4 tsp. green food coloring
4 C. corn flakes
1/4 C. small cinnamon candies

In a microwave safe bowl, heat butter and marshmallows on high for 2 to 3 minutes, stirring at the halfway point. Stir until smooth.

Add vanilla extract and green food coloring.

Place corn flakes in a large bowl and pour marshmallow mixture over the flakes. Stir thoroughly to combine and color each flake.

Grease hands. Shape 1/2 cup of the corn flake mixture on wax paper to form a wreath. Sprinkle with cinnamon candies.

Rudolph Cupcakes

Makes 24 cupcakes

24 paper baking cups
1 pkg. cake mix, any flavor
1 (16 oz.) tub chocolate frosting
Chocolate sprinkles
24 large pretzel twists
24 miniature marshmallows
24 red cinnamon candies
24 small red gumdrops

Prepare and bake cake mix according to package directions for cupcakes. Cool completely.

Frost cupcakes with frosting. Sprinkle chocolate sprinkles over tops of cupcakes.

For each cupcake, cut pretzel twist in half; arrange on cupcake for reindeer antlers. Cut miniature marshmallow in half; arrange on cupcake for eyes. Center gumdrop below marshmallow halves for nose. Place red cinnamon candy below gumdrop for mouth. Store loosely covered.

Heavenly Angels

Makes 24 servings

**24 white fudge covered chocolate
  sandwich cookies**
48 white Life Savers candies
24 yellow Life Savers candies
1 (16 oz.) tub vanilla frosting

Cut each cookie with sharp knife into 3 pieces. Wings should be about 3/8"
at widest part; body section should be about 1/2" at narrowest part.

Attach 2 white roll candies, one on top of the other, with frosting, for the
head. Attach yellow roll candy to head with frosting for the halo.

Arrange cookie pieces on sheet of wax paper in angel shape (cookies will
not touch at this point). Attach wings to angel body by piping on frosting
using the small star tip; fill in space between body and wings with frosting.
Attach head with frosting. Let dry.

Easy Santa Cookies

Makes 34 cookies

1 (18 oz.) pkg. refrigerated
   sugar cookie dough
2 C. powdered sugar
2 T. butter or margarine, softened
2 to 3 T. milk
2 or 3 drops red food coloring
68 semi-sweet chocolate chips
   (about 1/4 C.)
34 cinnamon candies or
   red mini M&M's
2/3 C. coconut
34 miniature marshmallows

Freeze cookie dough for at least 1 hour.

Preheat the oven to 350°F. Cut frozen dough into 1/4" slices. (Return dough to freezer if it becomes too soft to cut.) Place slices 3 inches apart on ungreased cookie sheets. Bake 8 to 12 minutes or until golden brown. Cool for 2 minutes. Remove from cookie sheets. Cool for 5 minutes or until completely cooled.

Meanwhile, in a small bowl, combine powdered sugar, butter and enough milk for desired spreading consistency; beat until smooth. Place half of frosting in a small bowl. Add red food color to one bowl; stir until blended.

Frost top 1/3 to 1/2 of cookie with red frosting for hat. Frost white semi-circle on other half of cookie. Use a small amount of frosting to attach chocolate chips for eyes and cinnamon candy or mini M&M's for nose. Gently press coconut into white frosting for beard. Press one marshmallow into red frosting for the end of Santa's hat. Let stand until frosting is set. Store between sheets of wax paper in tightly covered container.

Coconut Yule Trees

Makes 24 servings

3 C. flaked coconut
2 C. powdered sugar
1/4 C. butter or margarine,
    softened
1/4 C. light cream
1 tsp. almond extract
2 to 4 oz. dark chocolate
    candy coating
Green sugar
Red cinnamon candies

In a large bowl, combine the first 5 ingredients; mix well.

Drop by tablespoonfuls onto a cookie sheet lined with wax paper; chill for 1 hour. Shape into trees.

In a double boiler or microwave safe bowl, melt chocolate coating. Dip trunks of trees in chocolate and set on wax paper to harden.

Decorate tops of trees with green sugar and red cinnamon candies.

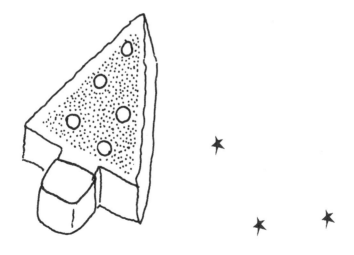

Rudolph Cookies

Makes 32 cookies

**4 (1 oz.) squares chocolate
candy coating
96 pretzel sticks
1 (16 oz.) pkg. Nutter Butter
cookies
64 blue, green or brown
mini M&M's
32 red mini M&M's**

Microwave chocolate candy coating in a small shallow glass dish on high for 3 minutes, stirring once.

Place 2 pretzel sticks in peanut butter filling of each sandwich cookie, forming large antlers. Break remaining pretzel sticks in half and place pretzel halves next to longer pretzel sticks, forming antlers.

Dip 1 side of blue, green or brown mini M&M's in melted candy coating and place, coated side down, on cookies for the eyes. Dip 1 side of red mini M&M in candy coating, and place on cookies, coated side down, for the nose.

Merry Santa Cupcakes

Makes 24 cupcakes

24 paper baking cups
1 pkg. white cake mix
1 (16 oz.) tub vanilla frosting
Red sugar crystals
Mini M&M's
Mini marshmallows

Prepare and bake cake mix according to package directions for cupcakes. Cool completely.

Frost each cupcake with vanilla frosting. Decorate each cupcake to look like Santa: for hat, sprinkle top third and halfway down one side of cupcake with red sugar crystals. Place mini M&M's on frosting for eyes and nose. Cut 2 mini marshmallows in half lengthwise, place at edge of red sugar for hat brim. Place one mini marshmallow at end of red sugar on side for the hat tip. For beard, place about 10 mini marshmallows over bottom third of frosting.

Wrap cupcakes in plastic wrap or store cupcakes in an airtight container.

Angel Cookies

Makes 36 cookies

**1 (18 oz.) pkg. refrigerated
   sugar cookie dough
72 small pretzel twists
Decorator sugar or regular sugar
Vanilla frosting**

Preheat the oven to 350°F. For easier slicing and shaping, work with half roll of well-chilled dough at a time; refrigerate remaining dough until needed. Slice dough into 1/4" slices.

For each angel, cut narrow strip from 2 sides of slice, forming a triangle. Roll strips into 1 ball. Place triangle on ungreased cookie sheet.

To form wings, place 2 pretzels on either side of top point of triangle, making sure single hole side of pretzels touches dough.

Place ball on top of triangle to form head; press with fingers to flatten. Repeat with remaining dough slices and pretzels, placing 2 inches apart on cookie sheets. Sprinkle with sugar.

Bake 7 to 11 minutes or until light golden brown. Cool for 1 minute; remove from cookie sheets. Pipe vanilla frosting around outside edges of cookie and around pretzel twists. Pipe on hair and continue to decorate as desired.

Reindeer Treats

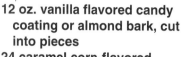

Makes 24 servings

**12 oz. vanilla flavored candy
coating or almond bark, cut
into pieces
24 caramel corn-flavored
miniature rice cakes
48 miniature pretzel twists
48 chocolate chips
24 red cinnamon candies**

Line cookie sheet with wax paper. In a medium saucepan, melt candy coating over low heat, stirring constantly.

For each reindeer, dip rice cake in candy coating; place on wax paper-lined cookie sheet. Dip rounded side of 2 pretzels in candy coating; place on each side of rice cake to resemble antlers.

Decorate with chocolate chips for eyes and cinnamon candy for nose. Let stand 15 minutes or until set. Carefully remove from wax paper; store in an airtight container.

Christmas Tree Brownies

Makes 15 bars

1 pkg. brownie mix
2 C. mini M&M's
1 (16 oz.) tub vanilla frosting
Green food coloring

Prepare the brownie mix according to package directions, but use a 15 x 10 x 1 inch baking sheet lined with foil and greased. Mix 1 cup of the mini M&M's into the batter. Spread brownie batter evenly to edges of baking sheet. Bake for 20 minutes. Cool completely.

Use a cookie cutter to cut out tree shapes; reserve extra brownie bits for snacking or crumbling over ice cream. Frost with vanilla frosting, tinted green with a few drops of food coloring. Decorate with more mini M&M's. Store covered or in an airtight container.

Christmas Tree Crispy Pops

Makes 20 servings

3 T. butter or margarine
1 (10 oz.) pkg. marshmallows
6 C. crispy rice cereal
Colored plastic wrap
Creamy frosting, tinted as desired
Assorted small candies
Candy canes
Assorted ribbons

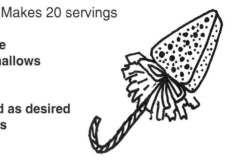

In a microwave safe bowl, heat butter and marshmallows on high for 2 to 3 minutes, stirring at the halfway point. Stir until smooth.

Add crispy rice cereal. Stir until well coated.

Using a buttered spatula or wax paper, press mixture evenly in 9 x 13 x 2 inch pan coated with cooking spray.

Cut tree-shaped triangles from the cereal treats. Frost one of the flat sides of each treat. Sprinkle or arrange candies on frosting. Let stand several hours to dry. Use the tip of sharp knife or large skewer to make a hole in base of each tree, being sure to center the hole in the base. Push straight end of a candy cane into each hole.

Tear off a sheet of plastic wrap about twice the size of each tree. Place top point of tree in center of wrap. Bring plastic wrap down around tree. Pinch plastic wrap together at candy cane, leaving ends of plastic wrap free. While pinching wrap, twist tree to seal plastic wrap.

Tie ribbon around twist to secure, being careful not to handle ends of plastic wrap too much. Gently fluff out ends of plastic wrap.

Raspberry Hearts

Makes 24 cookies

2 eggs, hard-boiled
3/4 C. unsalted butter
2 C. unbleached all-purpose flour
1/4 C. brown sugar
2 egg yolks
1 T. lemon zest
2 tsp. ground cinnamon
1 pinch salt
1 (8 oz.) jar seedless raspberry jam
2 eggs
2 T. water

Peel hard-boiled eggs and remove yolks. Press yolks through a sieve and set aside.

Cut the butter into small pieces. Add in the flour, brown sugar, egg yolks, hard-boiled egg yolks, lemon zest, cinnamon and salt in a mixing bowl. Mix with your hands until the dough holds together and all the ingredients are well blended. Wrap the dough in plastic wrap and refrigerate for at least 2 hours.

Roll out the dough 1/4" thick on a lightly floured surface. Using a 2 1/2 to 3" heart-shaped cookie cutter, cut out as many hearts as possible. Gather the dough scraps, reroll and cut out more hearts. Using a smaller heart-shaped cookie cutter, cut out the centers of half the cookies. Gather centers, reroll and cut out more hearts.

Preheat the oven to 350°F. Line baking sheets with parchment paper.

Spread each whole heart with a thin coating of raspberry jam. Top with the hearts with cut out centers. Repeat until all the dough has been used. Place the hearts 1" apart on the lined baking sheets. Beat 2 eggs with water in a small bowl and brush lightly over the cookie frames.

Bake the cookies just until light golden brown, 12 to 15 minutes. Cool on wire racks and store in the freezer or in an airtight container until ready to serve.

★ "I choo-choose you!" Cupcakes ★

Makes 24 cupcakes

24 paper baking cups
1 pkg. cake mix, any flavor
1 (16 oz.) tub vanilla frosting
24 tootsie rolls (the short kind)
24 toothpicks
Red licorice twists
12 miniature peanut butter cups
144 red cinnamon candies
1 tube red gel icing
White paper, markers and tape

Prepare and bake cake mix according to package directions for cupcakes. Cool completely.

Frost the cupcakes, reserving a little frosting to build the train engines.

For each engine, unwrap a tootsie roll and slice off 1/3 of its length (the tootsie roll is actually scored into 3 sections). Firmly press the short slice atop the back end of the remaining piece so that it sticks in place to create the train engine's body.

Use a toothpick to anchor a 1/2" piece of licorice to the top of the engine for a smoke stack. With a serrated knife, gently saw a peanut butter cup in half. Then attach one half, turned upside down, to the front of the engine to form a cowcatcher. Use frosting to stick 3 red cinnamon candies for wheels along the bottom of each side.

Set the engine on top of the cupcake and press it slightly into the frosting. Then use red gel icing to draw a train track in front and in back of the engine. Finally, cut out a paper steam puff. Print on the message "I choo-choose you!" And tape it to the top of the toothpick.

Valentine Crispy Cut-Outs

Makes 20 servings

3 T. butter or margarine
1 (10 oz.) pkg. marshmallows or
** 4 C. miniature marshmallows**
6 C. crispy rice cereal or chocolate-
** flavored crispy rice cereal**
Red decorating gel
Red cinnamon candies

In a microwave safe bowl, heat butter and marshmallows on high for 2 to 3 minutes, stirring at the halfway point. Stir until smooth.

Add crispy rice cereal. Stir until well coated.

Press mixture into 15 x 10 x 1 inch pan coated with cooking spray. When slightly cooled, cut into heart shapes using heart shaped cookie cutter. Write names on each heart with red decorating gel. Trim edges with red cinnamon candies, using frosting or decorating gel to hold candies in place.

Red Hearts

Makes 48 servings

1 C. shortening
2 C. sugar
2 eggs
1 tsp. vanilla
1 C. buttermilk
2 tsp. baking soda
4 1/2 C. all-purpose flour
3 drops red food coloring
Sugar

Mix ingredients in the order given. Divide dough and add enough red food coloring for desired shades of pink or red.

Refrigerate dough for 40 to 60 minutes.

Preheat the oven to 350°F. Roll out the dough and cut out with heart cookie cutters. Sprinkle with sugar. Bake for 11 minutes.

Holiday Presents

Makes 24 servings

3 T. butter or margarine
1 (10 oz.) pkg. marshmallows or
** 4 C. miniature marshmallows**
6 C. crispy rice cereal or chocolate-
** flavored crispy rice cereal**
Holiday sprinkles
Red string licorice

In a microwave safe bowl, heat butter and marshmallows on high for 2 to 3 minutes, stirring at the halfway point. Stir until smooth.

Add crispy rice cereal. Stir until well coated.

Press mixture evenly into 9 x 13 x 2 inch pan coated with cooking spray. When cooled, cut into 2" squares.

Decorate with holiday sprinkles and use red string licorice for ribbon. Best if served the same day.

Easy Sugar Cookies

Make with refrigerated sugar cookie dough.

Snowman

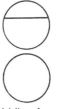 

Use 2 slices.

Using 1 slice dough, cut 1/3 for head and 2/3 for middle of snowman. Roll each into balls.

Place 2 balls, 1/2 inch apart, above whole slice to form snowman.

Angel

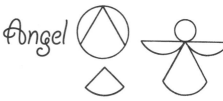

Use 1 1/4 slices.

Cut narrow strip from 2 sides of whole slice, forming a triangle.

Place 2 narrow strips on each side of top of triangle tip, for wings, inner edges touching and curved edges down.

Roll 1/4 slice into ball for head. Place at top to triangle.

Santa

Use 2 slices.

Cut narrow strips from 2 sides of 1 slice, forming a triangle.

Place triangle over 1 edge of whole slice for Santa's hat.

Place 2 narrow strips on whole slice for mustache, inner edges touching and curved edges down.

Add chocolate chip eyes.

Easy Sugar Cookies

Make with refrigerated sugar cookie dough.

Candy Cane

Use 1 slice.

Roll between hand to form about a 5-inch rope.

Shape into a cane.

Star

Use 1 1/4 slices.

Cut whole slice into 6 equal wedges for points of star. Roll 1/4 slice into ball for center of star.

Arrange wedges evenly around ball to form star, curved edges in and corners of wedges touching. (Wedges will not touch ball.)

Wreath

Roll 6 teaspoons dough into 6 balls.

Arrange balls 1/4 inch apart in a circle.

Everyday

Cookie Pops on a Stick

Makes 24 servings

2 C. butter or margarine, softened
1 tsp. baking soda
2 1/2 C. sugar
1 tsp. vanilla or other extract flavor
4 1/2 C. self-rising flour
24 wooden sticks

Preheat the oven to 350°F.

Combine butter, baking soda, sugar and your favorite extract flavor. Beat these ingredients together with an electric mixer until fluffy. Add self-rising flour. Beat well.

Roll dough into walnut sized balls. Place them 2 inches apart onto the cookie sheet and flatten slightly. Press ice cream stick into the flattened side of the cookie and press down. Add whatever decorations to each cookie you like, or, before pressing stick into the cookie, roll each cookie in sprinkles first, then flatten.

Bake until edges are lightly golden. Decorate baked cookies as desired.

School Days Pencil Cookies

Makes 24 to 30 cookies

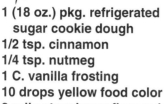

**1 (18 oz.) pkg. refrigerated
sugar cookie dough
1/2 tsp. cinnamon
1/4 tsp. nutmeg
1 C. vanilla frosting
10 drops yellow food color
2 rolls strawberry-flavored fruit snack
2 T. miniature semi-sweet chocolate chips
1/8 tsp. oil**

Preheat the oven to 350°F. Line 9 x 13 x 2 inch pan with foil. In a large bowl, break up cookie dough. Add cinnamon and nutmeg; knead dough with hands until well mixed. Press dough in bottom of foil-lined pan.

Bake 18 to 20 minutes or until edges are golden brown. Cool for 30 minutes or until completely cooled. Remove cookie from pan by lifting foil; remove foil.

Trim 1/2" off each short side of cookie. Cut cookie in half lengthwise. Cut widthwise each long strip into 3/4" wide strips. From one end of each 4 1/2" long "pencil" strip, cut off corners to form "pencil point." Discard corner pieces. Lay "pencils," bottom-side up, 1/2 inch apart on wire rack over sheet of wax paper.

In a small microwave safe bowl, combine frosting and food color; blend well. Microwave on high for 30 to 40 seconds or until frosting is melted and can be stirred smooth. Spoon frosting over "pencils," leaving "points" unfrosted and allowing frosting to drip down sides. If desired, smooth sides with knife.

Cut fruit snack rolls into 25 (1 1/2") strips. Save any remaining fruit snack for a later use. At end of each "pencil," place 1 strip on top and down sides of "pencil" to form "eraser." Cool for at least 30 minutes or until frosting is set.

In another small microwave safe bowl, combine chocolate chips and oil. Microwave on high for 45 to 60 seconds or until chocolate can be stirred smooth. Dip "pencil points" in melted chocolate to resemble "lead." Cool for 15 minutes or until chocolate is set.

Sprinkled Apple

Makes 6 servings

6 large apples
6 wooden sticks
6 C. white chocolate morsels
3 C. sprinkles, or more
  depending on size of apple

Clean apples and insert wooden sticks into the center of each apple at the stem end. Place on a sheet of wax paper.

Place white chocolate morsels in a microwave safe bowl. Microwave on medium power in 40 second intervals, stirring between each interval, until chocolate is thoroughly melted.

Spoon melted chocolate onto the apple to coat thoroughly.

Gently press sprinkles into the chocolate until the apple is thoroughly coated.

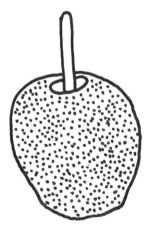

Striped Chocolate Apple

Makes 6 servings

6 large apples
6 wooden sticks
3 C. dark chocolate morsels
3 C. white chocolate morsels

Clean apples and insert wooden sticks into the center of each apple at the stem end. Place on a sheet of wax paper.

Place dark chocolate morsels in a microwave safe bowl. Microwave on medium power in 40 second intervals, stirring between each interval, until chocolate is thoroughly melted.

Spoon melted dark chocolate into a plastic squirt bottle and place the lid on tightly.

Squirt dark chocolate in up-and-down lines on the sides of the apple. Let dry.

Repeat the same process with the white chocolate.

ABC Snack Mix

Makes 20 servings

**4 C. frosted letter oat and
corn cereal, any variety
3 C. assorted festive candies
2 C. caramel popcorn
1 C. peanuts
1 C. small pretzels**

Other ingredients to use or for substitution: miniature marshmallows, chocolate chips, popcorn, mixed nuts, raisins, dried fruit or M&M's.

Mix all ingredients in a large bowl.

Use snack-size resealable plastic bags and place 1/2 cup mix in each bag. Or cut squares of colored plastic wrap and tie with colored ribbons.

Hamburger Cookies

Makes 20 servings

40 vanilla wafers
20 thin mint cookies (round)
1 tube green icing
1 tube red icing
1 tube yellow icing

Squeeze a little green, red and yellow icing around edges of thin mint cookie. Put one vanilla wafer on top and one on bottom of thin mint cookie so icing hangs out edges.

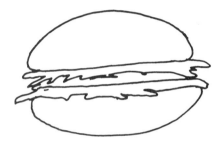

Crazy Cookie Creatures

Makes 18 cookies

1 (18 oz.) pkg. refrigerated
  sugar cookie dough
1/4 C. sugar
4 rolls fruit-flavored, ring-
  shaped hard candies
Candy corn
1 (16 oz.) tub vanilla frosting
Assorted paste or gel food color

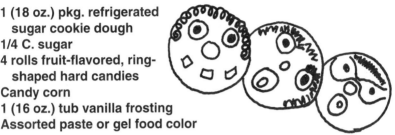

Freeze cookie dough for 30 minutes. Line 3 cookie sheets with foil.

Preheat the oven to 350°F. Cut chilled dough into 18 slices. Dip one side of each slice in sugar; place 6 slices, sugared side up, on each foil-lined cookie sheet.

Firmly press ring-shaped candies in dough for eyes (and, if desired, one for mouth). Press candy corn in dough for ears, horns, teeth, beak or mouth to create desired creature. (Be sure candies do not extend over edge of dough; they will melt onto cookie sheet.)

Bake 7 to 9 minutes or until edges are golden brown. Cool on cookie sheet for about 25 minutes or until completely cooled. Remove cookies from foil.

Meanwhile, divide frosting into small bowls. Add food color to each; blend until desired color. Place each color frosting in resealable plastic bag; seal bags. Cut small hole in bottom corner of each bag. Pipe on hair or glasses around the candies. Decorate cookies as desired.

Snappy Turtle Cookies

Makes 42 cookies

1/2 C. brown sugar
1/2 C. butter or margarine, softened
1/4 tsp. vanilla
1/8 tsp. imitation maple flavor,
   if desired
1 egg
1 egg, separated
1 1/2 C. all-purpose flour
1/4 tsp. baking soda
1/4 tsp. salt
1 C. pecan halves,
   split lengthwise
1/3 C. semi-sweet chocolate chips
3 T. milk
1 T. butter or margarine
1 C. powdered sugar

In a large bowl, combine brown sugar and 1/2 cup butter; beat until light and fluffy. Add vanilla, maple flavor, 1 whole egg and 1 egg yolk (save egg white); beat well.

Stir in flour, baking soda and salt; mix well. Cover with plastic wrap and refrigerate for about 1 hour for easier handling.

Preheat the oven to 350°F. Grease cookie sheets. Arrange pecan pieces in groups of 5 on greased cookie sheets to resemble head and legs of turtle. In a small bowl, beat egg white. Shape dough into 1-inch balls. Dip bottom in beaten egg white; press lightly onto pecans. Tips of pecans should show.

Bake 10 to 12 minutes or until edges are light golden brown. Immediately remove from cookie sheets. Cool for 15 minutes or until completely cooled.

In a small saucepan, combine chocolate chips, milk and 1 tablespoon butter; cook over low heat, stirring constantly until melted and smooth. Remove from heat; stir in powdered sugar. If necessary, add additional powdered sugar for desired spreading consistency. Frost cooled cookies. Let frosting set before storing. Store in tightly covered container.

Calico Kitty Cookies

Makes 24 cookies

1 (18 oz.) pkg. refrigerated
   chocolate chip cookie dough
48 pecan halves
72 M&M's
48 thin pretzel sticks,
   halved

Place cookie dough in freezer for at least 1 hour.

Preheat the oven to 350°F. Cut cookie dough into 24 slices. Place slices 3 inches apart on ungreased cookie sheets. For ears, press 2 pecan halves onto top of each cookie, overlapping edge of cookie. For eyes and nose, press in M&M's. For whiskers, place 2 pretzel halves on each side of nose; press in slightly.

Bake 11 to 13 minutes or until golden brown. Cool for 1 minute. Transfer to wire racks to cool completely.

Candy Train Engines

Makes 24 servings

24 pkgs. chewing gum,
  5 sticks each
96 round peppermint candies
24 rolls ring-shaped hard candies
24 foil-wrapped milk chocolate Kisses
24 assorted square or round foil-
  wrapped candies (Rolo's)
Glue gun and glue sticks

For each train engine, glue 4 peppermint candies for wheels onto the sides of a gum package.

Glue 1 roll of ring-shaped candies onto the gum package. Glue 1 chocolate Kiss and a foil-wrapped candy onto each end of the top of the engine.

Repeat to make remaining trains.

Chocolate Peanut Butter Frogs

Makes 12 frogs

2 (1 oz.) squares semi-sweet
  baking chocolate
2 T. butter or margarine
12 chocolate sandwich cookies
3 T. creamy peanut butter
24 miniature pretzel twists
24 M&M's

Place chocolate and butter in saucepan; cook over low heat until melted, stirring frequently; set aside.

Spread bottom of each cookie with 1 teaspoon of peanut butter; dip into melted chocolate mixture. Immediately press 2 pretzel twists on chocolate for frog legs with wide part of pretzels facing outward. Place, pretzel-side down, on wax paper-lined cookie sheet.

Attach M&M's for eyes using remaining chocolate mixture or peanut butter. Let stand until chocolate is set.

Crispy Pizza

Makes 12 servings

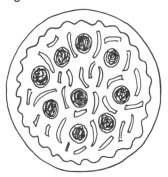

3 T. butter or margarine
1 (10 oz.) pkg. marshmallows or
  4 C. miniature marshmallows
6 C. crispy rice cereal or chocolate-
  flavored crispy rice cereal
Strawberry jam
Yellow frosting
Red fruit rollups cut into quarter-
  size circles

In a large microwave safe bowl, melt butter and marshmallows on high for 2 to 3 minutes, stirring at the halfway point. Stir until smooth.

Add crispy rice cereal, stirring until well coated. Spread cereal mixture into a 12 inch pizza pan coated with cooking spray. Allow to cool.

To make pizza, spread strawberry jam on top of cereal mixture for tomato sauce. Leave edges plain to resemble pizza crust. Put yellow frosting into a resealable plastic bag and cut a small hole in the corner. Squeeze frosting over strawberry jam for cheese. Decorate with fruit snack circles for pepperoni. Top with candy sprinkles as extra spices. Cut into 12 slices to serve.

Use your imagination when decorating the pizza. After spreading frosting onto cereal mixture, top with fruit slices or other candies.

Quickie Turtle Chippers

Makes 20 cookies

1 (18 oz.) pkg. refrigerated
chocolate chip cookie dough
100 pecan halves
24 Rolo's, unwrapped

Preheat the oven to 350°F. For each cookie, on ungreased cookie sheet, arrange 5 pecans to resemble head and legs of turtle. Top pecans with unbaked cookie (tips of pecans should show).

Bake 8 to 10 minutes or until golden brown. Immediately press 1 candy into top of each cookie. Cool for 2 minutes. Remove from cookie sheets; place on wire racks. Cool for an additional 4 minutes.

With knife, spread softened candy on each cookie into 2" round circle. Cool for 1 1/2 hours to set candy before storing in an airtight container.

Bacon and Eggs Candy

Makes 32 servings

96 small pretzel sticks
1 (1 lb.) pkg. white candy coating
64 yellow M&M's

Place white candy coating in a microwave safe bowl. Microwave on medium power in 40 second intervals, stirring between each interval, until candy coating is thoroughly melted.

Lay 3 pretzels side by side. Put a tablespoon of melted white candy coating in center to hold pretzels together and form the egg white.

Place 2 yellow M&M's in the center of white candy coating for yolks. Let harden at room temperature.

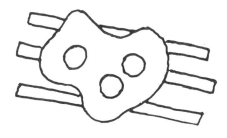

Caterpillars

Makes 12 servings

3 T. butter or margarine
1 (10 oz.) pkg. marshmallows or
4 C. miniature marshmallows
6 C. crispy rice cereal
1 (16 oz.) tub vanilla frosting
Mini M&M's
Black string licorice
Red string licorice

In a large microwave safe bowl, heat margarine and marshmallows on high for 2 to 3 minutes, stirring at the halfway point. Stir until smooth.

Stir in crispy rice cereal until well coated. Using spatula sprayed with cooking spray or wax paper, press mixture into a 15 x 10 x 1 inch pan coated with cooking spray.

Allow mixture to cool slightly. To make caterpillar sections, use a small round cookie cutter to cut cereal mixture into circles. Place 8 to 9 sections next to each other and use frosting to attach together to form caterpillar. Decorate using frosting to attach mini M&M's for eyes, black string licorice for antennae and legs and red string licorice for mouth on caterpillars. Decorate rest of body as desired.

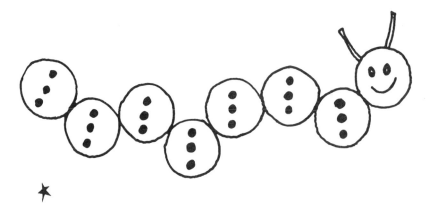

Dalmatian Cupcakes

Makes 24 cupcakes

24 paper baking cups
2 (3 oz.) pkgs. cream cheese,
  softened
1/3 C. sugar
1 egg
1 1/2 C. miniature semi-sweet
  chocolate chips
1 pkg. devil's food cake mix
1 (16 oz.) tub vanilla frosting

Preheat the oven to 350°F. Place paper baking cup in each of 24 muffin cups.

Beat cream cheese, sugar and egg in a medium bowl with electric mixer on medium speed until smooth. Stir in 1 cup of the chocolate chips; set aside.

Prepare cake mix according to package directions for cupcakes.

Divide batter among muffin cups (1/2 cup in each). Top each with 1 tablespoon cream cheese mixture.

Bake 20 to 25 minutes or until tops spring back when touched lightly. Cool for 10 minutes in pan. Remove from pan; cool completely, about 30 minutes.

Frost tops with frosting. Sprinkle with remaining chocolate chips.

Cute Pig Cookies

Makes 72 cookies

1 C. butter or margarine,
  softened
1 1/2 C. sugar
2 eggs
1 C. sour cream
1 tsp. vanilla
3 C. all-purpose flour
1 tsp. baking powder
1/2 tsp. salt
1/2 C. butter or margarine
4 C. powdered sugar
2 tsp. vanilla
6 T. milk
3 to 4 drops red food coloring
Pink sugar wafer cookies
36 marshmallows, halved
Mini chocolate chips

Preheat the oven to 375°F. Cream butter and sugar. Add eggs, sour cream and vanilla; mix well. Combine flour, baking powder and salt; add to creamed mixture and mix well.

Drop by tablespoonfuls onto ungreased baking sheets. Bake for 10 to 12 minutes or until edges are lightly browned. Cool on wire racks.

For frosting, melt butter. Add powdered sugar, vanilla, milk and food coloring; mix until smooth. Frost the cookies. Cut sugar wafers into triangles; place two on each cookie for ears. With a toothpick, poke holes in each marshmallow half for nostrils; press mini chocolate chips, tips down into holes. Place noses on the cookies. Add mini chocolate chips, tips up, for eyes.

Earth Worm Delights

Makes 24 servings

3 T. butter or margarine
1 (10 oz.) pkg. marshmallows or
  4 C. miniature marshmallows
6 C. chocolate-flavored
  crispy rice cereal
1 (2.75 oz.) pkg. gummy worms
3/4 C. chocolate sandwich
  cookie crumbs

In a large microwave safe bowl, melt butter and marshmallows on high for 2 to 3 minutes, stirring at the halfway point. Stir until smooth.

Stir in crispy rice cereal until well coated. Spread warm mixture into a 9 x 13 x 2 inch pan coated with cooking spray. Do not press firmly.

Arrange gummy worms over and around clumps of cereal. Sprinkle with cookie crumbs. Press crumbs lightly into cereal mixture. Cut into 2-inch squares when cooled.

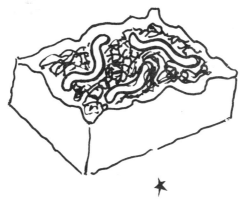

Clown Cupcakes

Makes 24 cupcakes

24 paper baking cups
1 pkg. cake mix, any flavor
1 (16 oz.) tub frosting, any flavor
24 marshmallows
48 mini M&M's
24 Hot Tamales
Red string licorice
Candy sprinkles, optional

Place paper baking cup in each of 24 muffin cups.

Prepare and bake cake mix according to package directions for cupcakes. Cool completely.

Cut a cone shape from the center of the cupcake for the clown's hat. Fill the hole in the cupcake with frosting and frost the top of the cupcake.

Place a marshmallow in the center of the cupcake. Put frosting on the top of the marshmallow, then place the cone shape piece of cupcake on top of the frosting.

Finish off with mini M&M's for eyes, a Hot Tamale nose and a red string licorice mouth. Sprinkle with candy spinkles of your choice, if desired.

Index

Spring

Summer

Fall

Winter

Everyday